Understanding
Massage

FIRST STONE

Contents

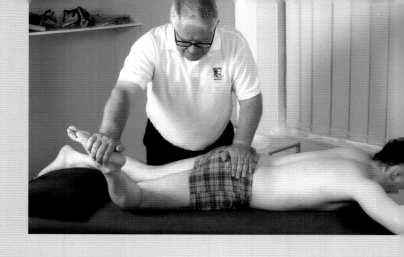

1

Understanding
The Therapy

Massage is probably the earliest form of medicine. It is based upon the manipulation of the soft tissues of the body, usually by the hands, for a therapeutic effect.

This is combined with the mobilisation of the joints upon which these tissues work.

Massage has a beneficial effect upon most musculo-skeletal conditions, for example, low back pain. But it is also suitable for many conditions that affect the muscles and joints of the body, including sports injuries. Massage can also form part of a treatment for those living stressful lives.

WHO INVENTED IT?

The origins of massage go back to the very beginnings of time. There are European cave paintings, depicting the use of massage, dating back to 15,000 BC. There is evidence to show that forms of massage were practised in China, India, Egypt, Israel and in other parts of the world many thousands of years ago.

Hippocrates is generally

Indian Head Massage is now one of the more popular of the massage therapies.

regarded as the Father of Medicine and he used a combination of massage, herbal remedies and nutrition in his treatments.

TYPES OF MASSAGE

There are many variations of massage. These include

- Therapeutic massage

Massage therapists, working at a sponsored bike ride. Massage therapy has an increasingly wide application and the benefits are proving to be far-reaching.

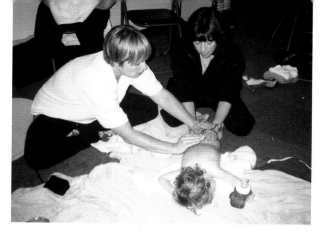

The benefits of baby massage are now widely acknowledged.

(relaxation massage)
- Remedial massage
- Aromatherapy massage
- Indian head massage
- Thai massage.

THERAPEUTIC MASSAGE
This type of massage, and many of the other variations, helps the recipient to relax, and to become less fraught and anxious.

REMEDIAL MASSAGE

This is an effective use of massage and movement to treat the many common musculo-skeletal problems that afflict the population. These may include:

- Spasm of the back muscles
- Disc problems
- Injuries to the major joints of the body (e.g. knee injuries, sprained ankles)
- Painful neck and shoulders
- Headaches
- Arthritic patients benefit greatly from remedial massage treatments.

Modern remedial massage traces its origins to Professor Ling (1776-1839) and Dr Metzger (1838-1909).

Between 1850 and 1930, massage became a popular and effective method of treatment applied in mainstream medicine for a variety of conditions.

Every hospital had a massage department. This was run by a massage sister, who instructed nurses on how to use massage techniques as a remedy for many of the ills suffered by patients.

WHO CAN BE HELPED?

Massage can be used to help people in different ways.

- One of the most noticeable effects of a massage treatment is that it helps to ease anxiety and tension, and enables the patient to relax.

- More than 100 hospitals in the UK employ massage therapists to give treatments to patients.
  These include patients in intensive care and often recovering from surgery; patients suffering long-term illness, such as arthritis and cancer, and pregnant mothers and newborn infants.

- Remedial massage is most helpful to those suffering from long-term back problems, arthritic joints, neck and shoulder injuries, stiff necks, tension headaches, plus many other musculo-skeletal conditions.

- Massage helps athletes and sports people to prepare for competition.

When it is used in the true remedial sense, massage will enable competitors to recover from the rigours of their sport and help in the treatment of many forms of sports injuries.

- Massage has even made its way into the work place. Seated massage is provided by a number of companies for their employees, to relieve workplace tensions and to engender feelings of well-being, thus improving efficiency and productivity.

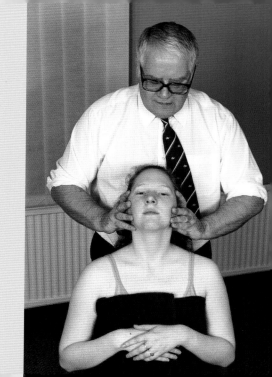

2 Backing Up The Claims

For centuries, most of the claims made regarding the benefits of massage were deemed to be anecdotal. They had no scientific basis; they were simply the reports handed down by patients and therapists over the years.

RESEARCH STUDIES

In recent times, this has changed, and there is now a growing wealth of evidence, coming mainly from university medical departments, to support the claims of the efficacy of massage treatments.

• Regular massage treatments not only reduce anxiety but they also enhance patterns of alertness and mathematical skills in the workplace.

This was reported in the *International Journal of Neuroscience* 1996 by Tiffany Field of the University of Miami Medical School. Field has initiated and replicated a very impressive array of research projects about massage at the Touch Institute, which is based at the University.

- There is a growing number of research projects that have demonstrated the usefulness and benefits of massage treatment
  - For pain reduction in arthritic patients
  - For depressed and bulimic adolescents
  - For chronic fatigue sufferers
  - For headache and migraine victims
  - For mothers (pre- and post-childbirth)
  - For the treatment of musculo-skeletal injuries sustained during sports events.

- Several recent studies have demonstrated the benefits of massage for patients with low back pain. For example, Michele Preyde reported in the *Canadian Medical Association Journal* (June 27; 2000) that massage treatments were shown to improve back function and reduce back pain, compared to other groups who received either postural education or a placebo of sham laser therapy. Another important research project was that of Cherkin, published in *Archives of Internal Medicine* (2001), which showed the effectiveness of massage compared to traditional Chinese acupuncture and self care in the treatment of chronic low back pain.

- The American Cancer Society's website states that everything surrounding massage:
  - A soothing environment
  - A human touch that is essential to life
  - A caring therapist
  - The comfort of prolonged attention
  - Relaxed muscles

all combine to make massage one of the most supportive and helpful complementary therapies available to cancer patients.

There is much research to support this statement, and massage therapy is used increasingly alongside orthodox medical treatments in hospitals and hospices to help alleviate the symptoms of this illness.

- The claim that premenstrual symptoms are often relieved by massage has been demonstrated by research projects, notably Hernandez-Reif (2000) and Dianne Polseno (2002).
  Both projects concluded that massage therapy is effective in decreasing symptoms of premenstrual syndrome and premenstrual dysphoric disorder.

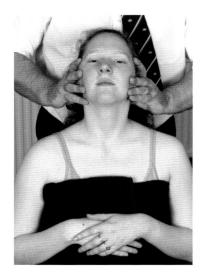

It has been found that massage reduces anxiety and stress, as well as treating physical conditions.

- Massage therapy appears to be an effective non-pharmacological treatment for alleviating chronic tension headaches. A significant and meaningful reduction in headache frequency and duration was observed in the study by Christopher Quinn and his colleagues, which was published in *Massage & Health*, (spring 2003).

- Currently, research projects are being carried out at several centres in Britain, including a combined project by the Northern Institute of Massage, the London and Counties Society of Physiologists (LCSP) Register of Remedial Masseurs and the Department of Community Nursing at the University of Central Lancashire.

3

Massage
Techniques

There are four major techniques of massage:

- **Effleurage**
- **Petrissage**
- **Frictions**
- **Tapotement.**

The masseur will use all (or a combination of) these techniques during a treatment session. The frequency and intensity will be varied according to the needs of the individual patient.

EFFLEURAGE
This is perhaps the best known and most used of all massage techniques. It is the stroke of initial contact with the patient and, as such, it is most important that effleurage is given with great skill.

Effleurage is usually performed with the whole palm surface of one or both hands.

It is mostly directed towards the heart, for example up the legs, up the back, but down the neck.

The pressure of the stroke should be applied in this one direction with the return stroke being very light.

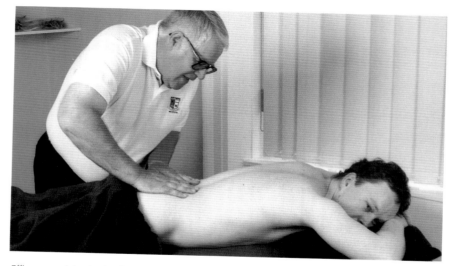

Effleurage of the back. This technique is usually performed with the whole palm surface of one or both hands. It is the most commonly used massage technique.

BENEFITS OF EFFLEURAGE

There are several benefits of effleurage:

- It helps to relax the patient
- It has a soothing effect upon tired muscles
- It assists the circulation of the veins and the return of blood to the heart and lungs
- It stimulates lymphatic drainage and helps to rid the body of toxic wastes
- Many patients report that massage helps them to sleep better.

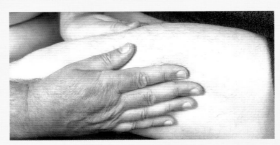

Hand position during effleurage of the thigh.

PETRISSAGE

The word 'petrissage' is derived from the French word 'to mash' or 'to knead' with the hands. Petrissage involves the systematic lifting and squeezing of muscles, lifting and rolling of muscles, kneading of muscles and wringing of muscles. The best way it can be envisaged is to compare it to wringing out a chamois leather.

BENEFITS OF PETRISSAGE

Petrissage benefits the patient by:
- Increasing the blood flow out of muscles via the veins
- Flushing out waste residue from muscles
- Loosening adhesions in muscles
- Stimulating blood flow into muscles, thus increasing the nutrition supply
- Helping to reduce muscular aches and pains.

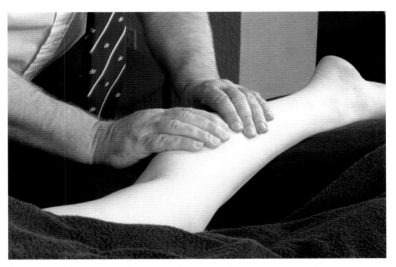

Petrissage of the calf muscles. This technique involves the systematic lifting and squeezing of muscles. It is best compared to a 'kneading' action.

FRICTIONS

The most common form of friction movements are performed by either the thumb(s) or fingers, in a series of circular movements applied to muscles and around joints.

Another technique is to friction across the fibres of ligaments and tendons.

This is often used in the treatment of sports injuries as well as to a variety of other injuries.

BENEFITS OF FRICTIONS

Frictions are helpful in several ways, as they:

- Generate heat in the tissues
- Dilate capillaries and help to stimulate the circulation
- Help to break down adhesions in muscles and around joints.

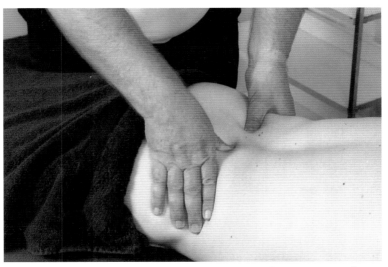

Frictions of the spinal muscles. This technique is often used for the treatment of sports injuries. The thumb or fingers are used in circular movements.

TAPOTEMENT

Tapotement techniques are used for a stimulating effect. When performed by a skilled therapist, they are indeed a pleasure to watch.

Tapotement includes the movements of clapping, hacking, flicking, beating, pounding and vibrational movements.

BENEFITS OF TAPOTEMENT

The benefits of tapotement are:

- It helps to tone the muscles
- It has a stimulating effect upon the circulation and upon the nervous system
- It is a very helpful technique for pre-event massage for sports people.

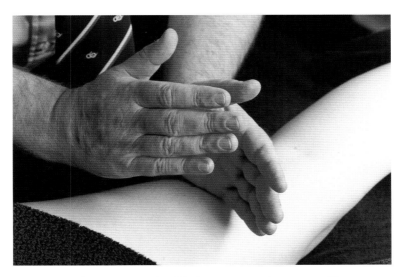

Tapotement techniques require the skill of an experienced practitioner. When used correctly, they have a toning and stimulating effect on the muscles.

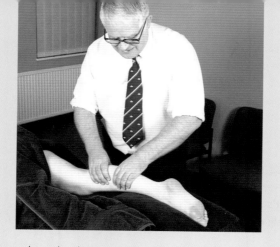

4 A Massage Treatment

It is not unusual that some people feel a little apprehensive about their first massage treatment. The trained therapist will quickly put the new patient at ease and will start by discussing the treatment.

The therapist will ask about the patient's medical history. It is absolutely essential to make sure that there are no contraindications to massage (see pages 34-35). Each new patient will be examined in the following way:

- Visually
- By palpation
- By testing the range of movement.

A treatment plan will be discussed and agreed upon by the therapist and the patient before any treatment begins.

THE PROCEDURE

The treatment room will be clean and warm. There should be a designated changing area to undress. There is never a need to remove underwear. The therapist will provide towels to wrap around the patient to

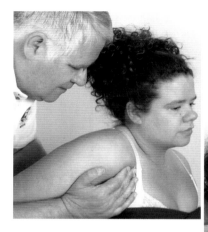

The practitioner will make a thorough examination by testing the patient's range of movement.

keep them warm and secure during the treatment, only exposing the part of the body that is being worked upon.

A full-body massage, which is used either to relax or to tone up the body, will take between 60 and 75 minutes.

More specific remedial massage treatments, e.g. a back treatment, will take between 25 and 45 minutes, depending on the needs of the individual patient and the skills of the therapist.

For joint and muscle conditions, more than one treatment will usually be required and the therapist will arrange follow-up appointments with the patient.

Many people appreciate the value of regular massage treatments. For some, this is a preventative measure to guard against future problems. Others simply enjoy the sense of relaxation and well-being that comes with each treatment.

This is something for the patient to discuss with the therapist, who will be pleased to suggest a maintenance plan.

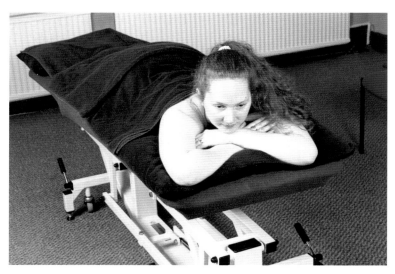

It is customary for the patient to be wrapped in towels during a massage treatment. Only the part of the body that is to be worked on is exposed.

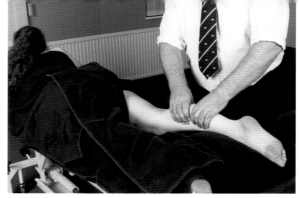

Massage creams provide good lubrication

OILS AND CREAMS

The principal function of any oils or creams used during a treatment is to reduce friction between the therapist's hands and the patient's body, thus allowing the massage movements to flow smoothly.

The use of oils is traditional in massage and long pre-dates modern aromatherapy. Oils can provide good lubrication but the use of essential oils without full training is not encouraged. If

33

these oils are not stored correctly, they can become unpleasantly rancid.

French chalk and talcum powder were in fashion many years ago but are not considered particularly good massage mediums nowadays.

Massage creams are more manageable than oils and provide good lubrication, with little mess on towels, white tunics and clothing.

A hypoallergenic lubricant is available, which will not trigger allergic reactions in the patient.

CONTRAINDICATIONS

Not everybody is suitable for massage treatment. There are good medical reasons why massage should not be performed on certain individuals, and the therapist will try to ascertain if any of these apply before commencing a treatment.

CONTRAINDICATIONS

The main contraindications include:

- Any contagious illness, such as measles or a skin condition
- No massage should be given over the site of recent surgery, wounds or burns
- Back or abdominal massage should not be given during the first three months of pregnancy or where there are menstrual problems
- Massage should not be performed over varicose veins
- Massage is not advisable in acute inflammatory conditions, e.g. acute arthritis, gastro-enteritis, acute appendicitis
- If patients are already receiving treatment for medical conditions, e.g. cancer, heart, vascular or kidney problems, the therapist would first seek the approval and permission of the patient's doctor or consultant before starting treatment
- No therapist would knowingly massage a patient who was under the influence of alcohol or drugs.

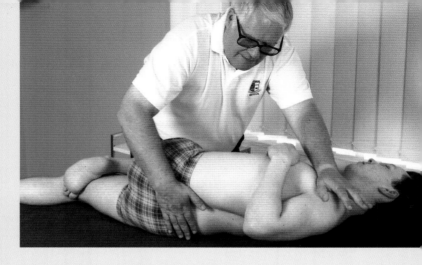

5 Case Histories

Without contravening the patient/therapist confidentiality relationship and with the patients' permission, there follows some accounts of how massage treatments have helped a variety of patients.

THE SECRETARY

Sarah is a secretary with many years' experience of typewriters and keyboards. She became aware of a gradual loss of movement in her neck, followed by aches and pains in the neck and shoulders. On occasions, these became so severe that she could not turn her head. She was also experiencing frequent headaches.

On examination, it became obvious that the muscles that connect the base of the skull to the spine and to the shoulders were in a state of chronic contraction and liable to go into cramp-like spasms.

Sarah received massage treatments to the neck and

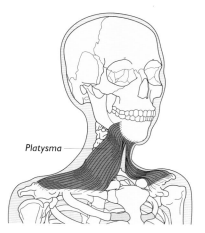

Platysma

The skill of the masseur can be better understood if we have some knowledge of where the muscles are located, and how they work. This illustration shows the platysma muscles of the neck.

shoulders, combined with special movements, which the therapist guided her through. She was asked to go through the routine that took her neck and shoulder joints through their range of movements several times each day.

She was also advised about her working position in front of the keyboard. As a result, Sarah altered the position of the keyboard and monitor, and adjusted the height of her chair.

Sarah received two treatments a week for three weeks and persevered with the gentle exercises each day. Her neck and shoulder muscles relaxed and movement became easier. The headaches and other pains disappeared during the course of the treatments.

Sarah now has a regular monthly treatment and has persuaded her firm to foot the bill in the interests of increased efficiency and employee health.

A PATIENT WITH LOW BACK PAIN

Alan was a furniture salesman, who travelled the country with his samples and spent much time each day loading and unloading his goods at shops, warehouses and exhibitions.

Alan telephoned one Saturday evening, just after six o' clock and, from the tone of his voice, it was obvious that he was in some distress with low back pain. The urgency was compounded by the fact that he was due to attend his parents' ruby wedding party that evening.

I saw Alan immediately and examination revealed that he was suffering from painful muscle spasm in the long muscles of the back. This makes any movement painful and difficult. I suspected that a combination of long-distance driving and heavy lifting had brought about this condition.

I treated Alan by giving his back a thorough massage, using mainly effleurage, petrissage and frictions.

In addition, I guided him through some movements that had the combined effect of easing his muscles and getting some movement back into the compressed spinal joints.

He was able to attend the celebrations at his parents' party without too much discomfort.

Alan attended for several more treatments; a single treatment for a long-term condition is never sufficient.

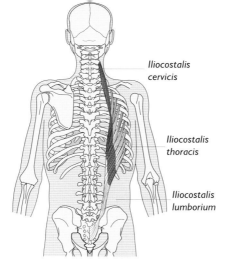

Iliocostalis cervicis

Iliocostalis thoracis

Iliocostalis lumborium

Back problems are widespread, and are more likely to affect people who have to do heavy lifting as part of their daily work. This diagram shows the iliocostalis muscles of the back.

However, after a course of treatments, his back had improved. We also discussed some suitable exercises that would mobilise his spine and keep his muscles well toned and relaxed. We talked about lifting techniques and also the dangers

41

of driving for long hours uninterrupted.

Between us, we agreed a plan to avoid any future episodes of severe low back pain, which included regular maintenance massage treatments that would act as a preventative measure.

This took place some 15 years ago and Alan still attends the clinic on a regular basis for his maintenance treatment. He remains free of major back pain.

PATIENTS WITH ARTHRITIS
Many arthritis sufferers benefit from regular massage treatments, and massage therapists treat many arthritic patients during their time in practice. The two main conditions are osteoarthritis (O-A) and rheumatoid arthritis (R-A). Between them, these conditions affect more than 10 million people in the UK.

OSTEOARTHRITIS
This is the most common form of the disease. It is a condition associated with the breakdown of the articular cartilage in a joint, notably the knee and the

hip. It causes pain, stiffness, loss of range of movement and, in some cases, deformity of the joint.

In a number of patients, the joints become so badly eroded and painful that replacement surgery is required.

RHEUMATOID ARTHRITIS
This is a painful, inflammatory illness that is systemic and symmetrical.

That is, it starts in the small joints of the hands and spreads, via the connective tissues, to affect other joints equally, on both sides of the body. In some cases, the disease spreads to the major organs of the body.

Treatment is usually by strong pharmaceutical drug therapy (which can have serious side-effects) and/or by surgery to replace badly damaged joints.

ARTHRITIS SUCCESS
Massage therapists treat patients with O-A with some confidence and with some success.

Sufferers of R-A often present great problems because of the severity of the condition. This is also one of the conditions where massage is contraindicated when the arthritis is in an acute or 'flare' stage.

CASE STUDY
During 2003, tutors at the Northern Institute of Massage came into contact with the Ramsbottom Branch of the Arthritis Research Council (ARC), and they decided to offer regular, specific treatments to seven women suffering from R-A – the more serious form of arthritis.

The offer was accepted, and each patient was given a thorough hand and arm massage once a month. This remedial treatment comprised the standard Northern Institute hand and arm massage of effleurage and petrissage of the whole arm up to the shoulder. This was followed by frictions around the joints and by passive movements of each finger joint and thumb joint, plus the joints of the wrist and elbow, followed by more effleurage. The treatment time was about 20 minutes for each patient.

The project, which is on-going, was reported in the *Bulletin of Massage Studies* (December 2002). This practitioner trial acted as a feasibility study to examine the need for massage treatments for rheumatoid arthritic patients and the following was noted:

- The patients, none of whom had previously received massage treatments, enjoyed the sessions and the social interaction with their colleagues and with the therapists

- They all felt that the treatments helped them to relax and feel less tense
- They reported that they felt less pain and discomfort in the days immediately following the massage treatments
- All the patients in the trial reported improvements in the ease and range of movements, of the joints of the fingers, wrists and elbows, and when performing daily tasks as a result of the massage treatments.

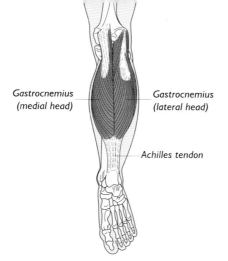

Gastrocnemius (medial head)

Gastrocnemius (lateral head)

Achilles tendon

A previous injury that has not healed correctly can often cause problems in later life when additional physical demands are made. This illustration shows the gastrocnemius muscles of the lower leg.

THE ATHLETE

David was an international athlete, whose speciality was fell racing. He was a national champion and he represented England on many occasions in international matches and at world championship events.

Many years previously, David had suffered a broken leg in a childhood accident and this left him with a leg length problem that, in turn, affected the muscles of his lower leg.

The result was that David often reported with injury and had to pull out of races. He was advised by a friend to have regular massage and that is how he became a patient of mine.

David came to see me with a plan already in his mind. He arranged to have massage treatments twice each week – one immediately before a race and then each Monday evening to help his recovery after the weekend's exertions.

The massage before the race was quite different to the after-race treatment. Before the race, the aim was to prepare his muscles for action so that, in combination with his warm-up routine, he would be at optimum fitness and readiness. These sessions were quite short but with the massage movements much brisker.

The Monday treatments were of remedial massage. These sessions were designed to clear accumulated toxic waste out of his system, to relax the muscles and to aid the natural repair processes of any minor injuries.

This treatment plan helped David with his running career for the next three or four years, and helped to keep him free of the injuries that had occurred in the past with such disappointing regularity.

SOCCER TEAMS

Many former students of the Northern Institute of Massage have found employment with professional soccer teams, including Liverpool and Everton, Newcastle United, Sunderland, Nottingham Forest, Middlesbrough, Blackpool, Carlisle United, Glasgow Rangers, Cowdenbeath, Rochdale, Bolton Wanderers, Portsmouth, Manchester City, Bury and Crewe Alexandra.

There has always been a place and a tradition for massage in soccer (and most other sports as well) but the influence of overseas players and coaches in the last 10 years has been significant.

Players now require massage on a daily basis as part of their preparation, training and, of course, when recovering from injuries.

This trend has spread to the semi-professional leagues and to many amateur teams. They have all experienced the benefits of regular massage treatments for enhanced performance and they have also seen a reduction in the incidence of injury among players.

David French, the masseur at Middlesbrough, recounts how he answered an advertisement and went along to the club where he was asked to perform leg massages on a couple of the apprentices.

Then came the real test: their most expensive signing, Fabrizio Ravanelli, the Italian international player, became the patient. David gave him a massage treatment to his legs and, literally, received the 'thumbs up' from Ravanelli upon completion of the treatment and was offered the job.

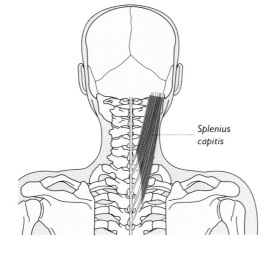

Splenius
capitis

When dealing with chronic headache, there are two areas to work on: the muscle attachments at the base of the skull, and the head itself. This illustration shows the splenius capitis muscle.

A PATIENT WITH CHRONIC HEADACHES

A man telephoned and asked if I would see his wife, who suffered from chronic headaches. These, she went on to tell me, had started 18 years previously when she was studying for her A Levels. She had got married and had children and was employed as a book-keeper for a chain of shops.

Throughout all this, the headaches were constantly there.

She had seen her doctor on many occasions and had taken various medications. She had been referred to the local hospital and had been examined by several doctors over the years. She had had two brain scans to determine if the cause was perhaps a tumour.

The headaches were worryingly constant and, intertwined with her family responsibilities and heavy work load, were making life unbearable. She appeared to have no other interests, hobbies or pastimes. Would massage help her?

The answer was an emphatic "yes" in her case. We agreed a plan to have two treatments a week for four weeks. On each occasion, a little like the secretary mentioned previously, she received a comprehensive massage treatment to the neck

51

and shoulders, combined with some gentle mobilising movements.

The treatment concentrated on the areas of the muscle attachments to the base of the skull. We also worked on the head itself and the muscles of the face and throat. The whole emphasis, at this stage, was on relaxing the muscles in particular and the patient in general.

At the end of the first treatment, she said very little and left quite quickly, and I was not sure whether the treatment had been successful. Three days later, she came for the second treatment. This followed the same procedure as the first session. Again, she remained quiet and non-committal.

As she entered the treatment room for the third treatment, she exclaimed that she had taken herself off her medication, and she had not had a headache of any kind for three days. She was delighted with the treatment and chatted away in a most uninhibited manner compared to her previous manner.

I suggested to her that she ought to go and see her GP rather than pick up the repeat prescription.

The doctor agreed that, pending a more permanent outcome, she could stay off her medication.

She came for the remainder of the treatments and obviously had a big re-think about her life style. She made some alterations to her working hours and responsibilities and she began to take much more exercise. I spoke to her again some three years after the last treatment and I literally had to jog her memory about her headache problem.

She had not had any further headaches and found it difficult to remember how badly they had affected her for so many years. Luckily for her, with the help of massage, she had managed to break the downward spiral of stress and headaches and was able to resume a more normal and healthy life.

A FROZEN SHOULDER
True 'frozen shoulder'

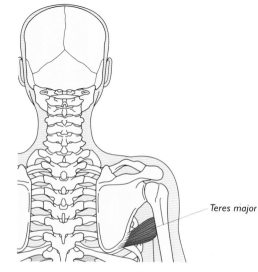

Pain in the shoulder can be very distressing, particularly when it is coupled with loss of movement. This illustration shows the teres major muscle.

Teres major

conditions, in which the patient cannot move the shoulder or arm on the affected side, are very rare. Many people do have shoulder pain that may result in a certain loss of movement and may describe the condition as frozen shoulder.

Mrs Fisher worked in the village shop. She came to the clinic for treatment because she was experiencing difficulty in reaching for items on the upper shelves, she could not 'peg out' on washing days, nor could she reach back for the safety belt in the car. She had been suffering for some weeks and had been taking analgesic tablets but they upset her tummy.

Mrs Fisher received four massage treatments and, after the first session, she was asked to perform some gentle exercises to mobilise both shoulders each day.

The treatments were a success and, for the next few months, Mrs Fisher acted as an unpaid, unofficial but very effective ambassador for the clinic. She told all her customers, who had listened to her tale of woe for many weeks, how good the massage treatments had been and that her shoulder had been 'cured' at long last.

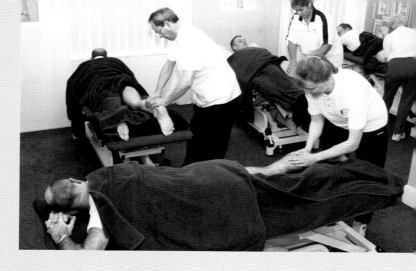

6 Learning How To Massage

Many people, often as a result of experiencing an expert massage treatment, express a desire to train as therapists themselves. There are so many courses available that the choice can be bewildering. Which course is best for you?

BODY MASSAGE

Many of the courses offer basic body massage, with some anatomy and physiology. If your time is limited or if all you want is to be able to give a relaxing body massage to family members or friends, then these courses are fine.

Many local authority colleges of further education offer short courses in body massage, usually presented by the hairdressing and beauty therapy department.

REMEDIAL MASSAGE

If you wish to practise massage more seriously or even make it your career, you need to select much more carefully. You must choose a course that will qualify you to a professional standard, and make you eligible to join a professional society, like the LCSP Register of Remedial Masseurs and Manipulative Therapists.

REGISTRATION

The massage school should be registered with the General Council for Massage Therapy, the official national governing body for all massage therapists in the UK. The LCSP Register, which is also affiliated to the General Council for Massage Therapy, is the oldest and biggest professional association for massage therapists. It has more than 2,000 members in the UK, and many more in Ireland, North America, Europe and Australia.

Additionally, the course provider should also be able to offer you support after qualifying and a programme of Continuing Professional Education once the basic qualification is achieved.

COURSE CONTENTS

Courses generally take between 12-15 months and are a

combination of theoretical home study and attendance at a tuition centre for practical instruction.

The content of the course will include anatomy, physiology and pathology, patient handling, examination procedures, massage techniques, working with other health professionals, medical law and ethics, and instruction about setting up in business.

The Northern Institute of Massage even has a business advisor from the Inland Revenue on hand, to advise new therapists about taxation matters.

The practical classes are usually at weekends to enable prospective therapists to continue with their day jobs while taking the course.

Further Information

TO FIND A QUALIFIED MASSAGE THERAPIST

The Organising Secretary
The LCSP Register of Remedial
Masseurs & Manipulative
Therapists
330 Lytham Road
Blackpool
Lancashire
FY4 1DW

Telephone: 01253 408443
Website: www.lcsp.uk.com

THE NORTHERN INSTITUTE OF MASSAGE

Massage Therapy and Remedial Massage has been taught at the Northern Institute of Massage for nearly 80 years. Graduates mostly set up their own private practices but many others find employment in private health clinics, the NHS, hotels, leisure centres, cruise liners and with sports clubs, both professional and amateur.

The Northern Institute of
Massage
14-16 St. Mary's Place
Bury
Lancashire
BL9 0DZ

Telephone: 0161 797 1800
Website: www.nim56.co.uk
Email: information@nim56.co.uk

BOOKS TO READ

Remedial Massage Therapy
by Eddie Caldwell
Published by Corpus Publishing

Dance and Dancers' Injuries
by Chris Caldwell
Published by Corpus Publishing

Sports Therapy
by James Briggs
Published by Corpus Publishing

Seated Acupressure Massage
by Patricia Abercromby and
Davina Thompson
Published by Corpus Publishing

Indian Head Massage
by Kush Kumar
Published by Corpus Publishing

About the author

Eddie Caldwell is the Principal
of the Northern Institute of
Massage and the author of
Remedial Massage Therapy.
He has been a remedial
massage and manipulative
therapist and teacher for more
than 20 years, and lives in
Lancashire, near to the
Northern Institute at Bury in
Lancashire.

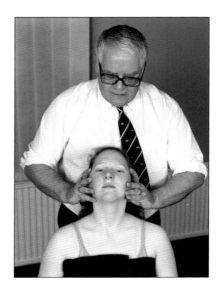

Other titles in the series

- **Understanding Acupressure**
- **Understanding Acupuncture**
- **Understanding The Alexander Technique**
- **Understanding Aromatherapy**
- **Understanding Bach Flower Remedies**
- **Understanding Echinacea**
- **Understanding Evening Primrose**
- **Understanding Feng Shui**
- **Understanding Fish Oils**
- **Understanding Garlic**
- **Understanding Ginseng**
- **Understanding Head Massage**
- **Understanding Kinesiology**
- **Understanding Lavender**
- **Understanding Pilates**
- **Understanding Reflexology**
- **Understanding Reiki**
- **Understanding St. John's Wort**
- **Understanding Shiatsu**
- **Understanding Yoga**

First published 2003 by First Stone Publishing
4/5 The Marina, Harbour Road, Lydney, Gloucestershire, GL15 5ET

ISBN 1 904439 06 3

Printed and bound in Hong Kong through Printworks International Ltd.